Piano Time Jazz Duets

Book 2

Contents

I just want to say . . .	2
Swing's the thing	4
All I want	6
Wrong number	8
Sassy	11
Dreamy beguine	14
Rags to riches	16
Moonlight waltz	18
Rampage	20
Giving it the works!	23
Follow the blues	26
Still	28
The Gambler	30
Boogie-woogie-hoogie	32
Hard cheese	35
Bossa cinco	38

Pauline Hall

MUSIC DEPARTMENT

OXFORD
UNIVERSITY PRESS

T0056059

I just want to say . . .

Alan Bullard

I just want to say . . .

Swing's the thing

Alan Haughton

Medium swing (♫ = ♪♪)

mf

5

cresc. *f* *p*

10

mf *f*

15

mf

20

cresc. *f* *sub. p*

Swing's the thing

Alan Haughton

Medium swing (♫ = ♪♪)

mf

5 *cresc.* *f* *p*

10 *mf* *f*

15 *mf*

20 *cresc.* *f* *sub. p*

All I want

Peter Gritton

All I want

Peter Gritton

Wrong number

Pauline Hall

Swing (♫ = ♩³♪)

mp

Primo

It seems to me we're on the wrong wave - length, when -

Swing (♫ = ♩³♪)

Secondo

mp

3

- ev - er I want to talk to you; and i - ma-gine my frus-tra-tion when there's

6

no com-mu - ni - ca-tion, ev - en if it's just to say we're through.

9
mf
Wrong num-ber, that's what I al-ways get, the wrong num-ber, I some-how seem to get the
mf
13
wrong num-ber ring-ing when I try to call you. If
f
16
on-ly I could talk to you I know I'd feel O-K, when you an-swered the phone. You
f

20
seem so far a-way, I can't make you un-der-stand what it's like to be a - lone.
24
mp
Wrong num - ber, it's al - ways just the same, the wrong num - ber,
mp
rall.
slower
27
p
and who's to blame if it's the wrong num-ber ring-ing when I'm miss-ing you!
rall.
slower
p
pp

Sassy

Steve Milloy
With attitude! (♫ = ♪³♪)
Primo
With attitude! (♫ = ♪³♪)
Secondo
mf
5
8va
mf
mp
9
(8va)

(8va)
13
mf
(8va)
17
loco
mp
p
21

25
f
f
29
8va
mf
mp
(8va)
33
ff
ff

Dreamy beguine

Denis McCaldin

Dreamy beguine

Rags to riches

Alan Haughton

Rags to riches

Alan Haughton

Moonlight waltz

Stephen Duro

Moonlight waltz

Rampage

Charles Beale

13
f
17
mf
5
mf
21
(optional E–G roll)

24
29
8va

BASIN ST.

Giving it the works!

13
17
8va
21
(8va)

24
(8va)
ff
al - le-lu - ia!
f
ff
al - le-lu - ia!
f
27
(8va)
30
(8va)
Slower
loco
ff
Slower
ff

Follow the blues

Alan Bullard

Follow the blues

In the first section the right hand *either* copies the left hand (an octave higher) *or* improvises.
In the second section the hands are reversed!

Alan Bullard

Still

Charles Beale

Flowing

p

con Ped.

6

11

mp

16

21

mf

27

pp

dim.

molto rit.

ppp

Primo

Still

Charles Beale

Flowing

p

6

11

mp

16

21

mf

p

27

pp

dim.

molto rit.

ppp

The Gambler

Nikki Iles

The Gambler

Boogie-woogie-hoogie

This energetic boogie can be played either straight or swung (♫ = ♩³♪)

Roderick Williams

12
cresc.
f
cresc.
f
16
sub. p
(cheekily)
f
sub. p
(cheekily)
f
21
meno f
f
meno f
f

26
mf
cresc.
mf
cresc.
30
sub. meno f
sub. meno f
34
mp
p
dim.
mp
p

Hard cheese

The pupil plays Secondo in this funky duet. The RH melody in bars 13–20 is optional.

10
fp
f
ff
ff
13
pp
(RH optional until bar 21)
pp
17
mf
mf

21
fp
f
f
24
ff
ff
ff
27
mf
ff
mf
pp
ff
8vb

Bossa cinco

Roderick Williams

Easily flowing

Primo

p semplice

Easily flowing

Secondo

p

mf espress.

7
11
cresc.
f dim.
mf
cresc.
f dim.
p
15

19
cresc.
cresc.
22
f
dim.
f
dim.
25
p
p